Anxiety

BY DEREK O'NEILL

Copyright © 2018 by Derek O'Neill

For information about permission to reproduce excerpts from this book write to:
Derek O'Neill
244 5th Avenue, Suite D-264
New York, NY 10001
E-Mail: info@derekoneill.com

ISBN: 978-1-936470-95-2
First Edition

All rights reserved, including the right to reproduce this work in any form whatsoever (audio, visual, electronic, etc.). Such reproduction is expressly forbidden without permission in writing from Derek O'Neill, except for brief passages in connection with a review. It is not the intent of the author to offer advice in any form, whether it is spiritual, psychological, medical, or other. If you are in need of special assistance or advice, please consult with a proper professional. The information within this book is offered as an avenue to inspiration and awareness. This book does not claim to possess all the answers, nor to heal or counsel. If you choose to apply the principles within this book to your life, that is your constitutional right.

Get a Grip Series © 2018
Editor: Nancy Moss
Front Cover Design: Derek O'Neill

DEDICATION

To all who read this book, I salute you for wanting to change the way you live for the better and for having the courage to be who you are as fully as possible.

To all who encourage me every day to keep going and sharing their lives with me, family small and large. But most of all the little angels who came to teach me – Alexa, Blake and Calvin, my grandchildren.

"Everybody hurts sometimes, and when we do it is nice to have Derek O'Neill around. His excellent little books on the things that get us, (fear, anger, depression, victimhood, mental blocks) allow us to find our way safely through our psychological minefields and arrive safely at the other side. Read them when you need them."

Paul Perry, Author of the
New York Times Bestseller
Evidence of the Afterlife

TABLE OF CONTENTS

Dedication .... *iii*

Author's Preface .... *ix*

Understanding Anxiety – The First Step To Serenity 1

Is Anxiety A Habit? 8

Anxiety As A Messenger 14

Your Past – The Roots Of Anxiety 23

Anxiety And The Fear Of Lack 29

Anxiety In A Chaotic World – Acceptance, Healing And Hope 34

Practical Tips To Combat Anxiety 40

Meditation To Ease Anxiety 48

About The Author *55*

AUTHOR'S PREFACE

Thank you for purchasing *Anxiety: To Peace*. This book has not come about as a result of my training as a therapist, but through some hard-earned lessons that I have experienced myself. This is how I know the path out of limiting beliefs and behaviors that hinder growth. The tools that I offer in this book have worked not only for me, but also for hundreds if not thousands of other people. I have shared these ideas and techniques in my workshops, one-on-one sessions, video and radio broadcasts, and on my website, and I have witnessed astounding results time and time again. Through observation of others, and myself, I have learned to identify the triggers and root causes of disharmony. Most of all, I have come to understand and apply the best methods for achieving peace and balance in life; not perfection, but real transformation and harmony that comes with learning who we are and what makes us tick. My 35 years of martial arts study has given me a refined sense of timing for when to strike with the sword to cut away old patterns, and when to use the brush to paint the picture of the life we deserve and can have.

The 'Get a Grip' series of books offers tangible, authentic wisdom that can help you in all aspects of your life. You've made a great choice by investing in this book. Enjoy the read, and take time to learn and apply the techniques. Let's change who we are together.

Derek

Anxiety
To Peace

UNDERSTANDING ANXIETY – THE FIRST STEP TO SERENITY

We have all experienced anxiety in one form or another. You might only feel it occasionally, when anticipating an unwelcome event or stressful situation. It may arise on a regular basis, like anticipating morning traffic or an encounter with a person in your life who demands a lot from you. Some people live with a certain level of anxiety nearly all the time, whether it be low-grade and in the background of their daily lives, or pronounced enough to be a problem that gets in the way of happiness and peace of mind. Anxiety shows up as tension, fear, worry, panic, and a host of other emotions. We can feel overwhelmed and think it will never let up. It can cause us to act against our own well-being. It can lead to physical and psychological complications. Our body and mind can feel weakened, muddled, or immobilized.

Anxiety, especially in these challenging times, may seem unavoidable, but if we change our perspective and way of thinking, anxiety doesn't have to stop us in our tracks. There is no magic formula for making anxiety disappear, but understanding it and to an extent, accepting it, is the route to releasing its hold on us. The goal of this little book is to give you the keys to that journey so you can start to change the dynamic of the anxiety that may be keeping you from experiencing joy and living a full life. Feeling anxious and being worried doesn't solve the problems you are anxious and worried about! Ironically, they only make them more challenging for you.

What is anxiety? Is it just another word for stress? Anxiety and stress may seem similar but think of anxiety as the sensation – sometimes long-term – that stress leaves you with. There are three different ways that anxiety appears in our lives, and often they intersect. The first is the emotional manifestation of anxiety; our feelings that occur as reactions to people, places and things, whether ongoing or new.

The second is psychological anxiety that is rooted in what has happened to us in the past, how we were raised, and events that have transpired in our lives. Everyone brings their baggage with them into stressful situations. We all know someone who seems to have very little anxiety no matter what is thrown their way. Maybe that person is you! Our orientation, our triggers, our emotional scars, all play a role. Having a difficult past can actually provide a road map for coping that helps you be less anxious, perhaps bringing a hard-earned consciousness to everything you face. It will be different for each person, yet we are ALL capable of dealing with the past and moving on as best we can.

The third kind of anxiety is physical, both when it is caused by physical/chemical issues (for example, a physiological predisposition for panic attacks, or other medical conditions), or the source of physical problems, which is so often the case when persistent stress shows up in the body. Even when the manifestation of anxiety is a "panic attack", triggered by something organic in the body, the role of your mind is often overlooked. Thoughts can create a chemical release. The domino effect of thinking yourself into a state of anxiety can turn into a deeper, chronic problem.

Anxiety can be what happens when fear meets stress and collides. When something triggers a fear that you have been carrying around with you and building in your subconscious, eventually a reaction might happen. No matter how stable you are, anxiety can cause your mind to focus on the fear, losing perspective of its context. Maybe you are losing something or someone that you allowed to define you, and now your identity – how you see it – is slipping away. Perhaps you are embarking on something new that you have terrible doubts about because of the way you perceive yourself. The source of anxious panic could be connected to abuse you suffered, or a stifling of your power. These are all real reasons, but they also manifest in your thoughts and attitudes.

The next time you feel anxiety rising, or turning into a panic attack, try to stop and ask yourself, "What is the source of this feeling?" Sit quietly and allow yourself to focus on understanding the anxiety, rather than experiencing the anxiety. We don't have to fight the feelings, rather we gently shift them to an orientation of reflection. You may be thinking that being able to understand your anxiety and examine it while you are in the thick of it will be very challenging. Remember that the smallest move towards connecting with the real reasons you feel panic or anxiety will open a path. It is not something that happens quickly and immediately changes everything. Understanding anxiety, in the bigger context and in your own life, will take a commitment. But just pausing, and looking at your feelings can be transformative.

Recognizing anxiety can be tricky, yet it's important. Sometimes there's a clear path to the cause and effect of it, for example, when you have a test in the morning and you have left the studying for the night before. Or perhaps you're about to meet your partner's very judgmental parents for the first time. It's obvious why you may feel anxious! More often than not our anxiety is complicated, subtle or insidious. We could have persistent anxiety about our jobs, our relationships, our family members, and/or our future. Emotions that we might not know we're feeling can arise as anxiety. We could be angry about something we've repressed – but it appears as anxiety. It could even be something that is a potential source of happiness for us, such as having feelings for someone we don't feel secure enough to express to them, causing us to have anxiety when in their company. All of these scenarios speak to consciousness and understanding. If our self-awareness is obscured or buried by denial or avoidance, anxiety acts as a mask and makes us miserable. If we are clear about what we are feeling and why, anxiety may still arise, but not with a profound or lasting effect. When we are attached to anxiety we can never dig deeper into our psyche and affect change. Feeling anxious, worried, or fearful becomes a counterproductive coping mechanism that can feed upon itself. Going "down the rabbit hole" of our negative thinking is usually accompanied by a big dose of anxiety!

IS ANXIETY A HABIT?

There's no denying that anxiety is real and that it manifests from actual situations, events, past history and dynamics. We also have to look at anxiety from another angle. It is a learned behavior. When we feel anxious, we are dipping into our personal storehouse of responses to triggers, and that becomes a habit. Anxiety may on a rare occasion stop us from acting on something we should steer clear of and think about, but for the most part, anxiety is causing us to put a barrier between ourselves and the ability to look at something with a clear head so we can figure out what triggered our feelings. When low-grade, constant anxiety grips us, we might not even realize it is there or what it does to keep us from our full potential.

How do we unravel and stop the anxiety habit? The first step is to accept that feelings will arise. Anxiety is natural, but we can learn to let it go. If we grasp at anything, we only feel its impact more, or create the opposite of what we would like. When we grasp anxiety, we are attached to what caused it, whether we know it or not. The key is to give situations or challenges the appropriate attention. If you "don't give it energy" and pretend it doesn't exist, you'll only push it down further into your subconscious where it is sure to pop up in a way that will not serve you well. On the other side of the coin, if you put too much focus and energy into your situation, you'll be giving it a life and power it doesn't merit. It is important to remember that feelings change and dissipate, whether because with time you gain perspective, or because the thing causing you anxiety shifts and evolves. Remembering the impermanence of everything in our lives is helpful as we apply it to anxiety. Even the darkest of problems change over time. When we've created a habit of anxiety it can become a persistent problem, causing us layer upon layer of new anxiety and confusion.

Once we accept our feelings of anxiety, we can learn not to grasp onto them. Applying the lessons of duality, and the fact that the pendulum of life will always swing back and forth between positive and negative, can ground us and awaken us from going down a path of anxiety. The goal is to achieve a state of processing anxiety by neither grasping it, nor meeting it with aversion. Both will lead to more suffering. Like with other emotions, there is a welcome you can give anxiety – a recognition to identify it, allow it to be, understand it, and then to let it pass. If you push anxiety down, it will only rise again.

Learning from our anxiety involves stopping and looking inward. Meditation can be a very useful tool for this but we can adopt a way of processing and understanding anxiety at any point in our day. Anxiety is the equation of exterior circumstances plus what your mind (and experiences in the past) bring to the table. With deeper understanding of your triggers, and how you habitually react, you can detach from a cycle of anxiety. Also remember that habits form as protection and coping mechanisms, though not ones that help you in the end. Be kind with yourself. Know that going deeper into your mind, and learning to make the choice to control it, is a journey, not a quick fix. You have to commit to do the work and break habits that do not serve you, and approach a new practice with self-love.

Thousands of thoughts go through the average mind in 24 hours. How many are negative and how many are positive? How many will cause some level of anxiety? It depends. Your first thought in the morning will probably affect where your mind will go the rest of the day. If you wake up thinking, "Aww, not another day!", the universe is going to greet you with, "Yes! It is one of those days again!" If you wake up with, "I am so grateful to be still breathing on this dimension!", the universe is going to show you the potential and beauty in everything. If we bring our minds to a place of neutrality, we allow feelings and thoughts to move through in an accepting way that doesn't feed anxiety. The only difference between somebody who is suffering with anxiety, and a master who has overcome it, is that the master has learned how to liberate their thoughts. If you create an endless cycle of grasping and aversion, hope and fear are constantly at battle with one another. The clashing dynamic between hope and fear manifests anxiety.

In order to shape your future, you have to be in a state of surrender. How does that work? It begins with opening your mind to awareness and consciousness. We empower ourselves to be positive or negative. Some people thrive on being negative because they actually think they don't know any other way. There's always another way, and a different point of view. It takes courage to shift your point of view. You have to look at how you may be stuck in the past, or in a belief that you carry that isn't realistic. Is your anxiety the result of being triggered by certain situations, or events and people from the past? Are you still being triggered by them? Are you still working on the reward and punishment program that was perhaps taught to you by your very loving and caring parents? These are things that are very much in your power to change.

ANXIETY AS A MESSENGER

While it is important to become aware of the connection between anxiety and the circumstances that brought it about, finding the trigger for the anxiety is just the beginning. Not only is it possible to explore what your subconscious and past history brings to the mix of anxiety, we can also look at what it may be telling us. Anxiety is a messenger that provides insight that may help alleviate the suffering it brings, and it also gives you tools to deal with other feelings and emotions such as fear, anger, depression, and problems with addictions. People develop compulsions that seem like a relief from anxiety, but actually put them on a vicious cycle that never allows for pleasure.

What are the underlying issues that you keep avoiding? Is feeling anxious in an unspecified way covering up what the emotion is trying to point out to you? Are you uneasy with the way you are responding to something? Instead of confronting it, are you shoving it down and squashing its voice? Do you self-medicate with alcohol or drugs because it makes you feel calm, only to have more anxiety the next day? Do you use relationships or work as a distraction instead of going deeper and looking at what makes you tick? Listen to your anxiety. Give it space to speak to you. You can defuse it and look at it for what it is. We know on a conscious level that anxiety is not going to change our situation, and can in fact make it worse, yet we allow it to infiltrate our mood, affecting our energy and our essential well-being. The message that anxiety brings can help you look at who you are, what is holding you back, and what you need to address in your approach to life. Again, your mind is manifesting your world. No matter what factors or circumstances you are facing, your response is under your control.

When you feel anxiety ask yourself, "Why have these events arrived for my enlightenment?" That's what events are for – your enlightenment. They're not here to harm you. YOU can harm you. When you are facing a challenge, especially when someone in your life is the trigger for your anxiety, you can decide not to put more energy into it, and do so without judgment towards yourself or others. There is an ultimate truth from the higher place within you. But you have to march through the external physical application of your manifestation. In the case of a person, it's not somebody doing something to you, it is you manifesting something because the seeds of conditions have arrived for the flourishing of this event for your enlightenment. From there, you achieve understanding and a way to process a situation, without anxiety.

Greeting anxiety with a "thank you" may seem odd, but when you process anxiety from a clear space, appreciating its message, your mind will begin to tell you what action you need to take in order to neutralize stressful events and change the dynamic that could be causing them. Don't judge anxiety. Treat it as a clue that is neither positive nor negative, but something that needs an adjustment. Anxiety is like a pressure gauge that is telling you the levels are wrong and you need to release the valve. And you are going to have to keep adjusting that valve as you move forward. That is the balance of life. Messages arrive to tell you that something you're doing is out of alignment with your highest good.

When you let go of the idea of fixing things, you realize that adjusting your mind is the only real "fix." The same is true for wishing that something or someone would be different. Again, feelings and reactions are what you CAN experience differently. We so often fall into a trap of thinking we can control the external world. A lot of unhappiness and suffering springs from the fruitless effort to do so. However, by working on your mind, your perspective, your actions and your sense of self – you turn the key to lasting joy, no matter what your circumstances are.

Every day, things happen all around us that try to trick us into thinking we can control the uncontrollable. You are continually being offered the opportunity to shift your thinking. Stop and realize that you don't control external things. You can't control a single thought in another person's head. You can't control the fact that your plane is late, your bus is making every stop, or that your car breaks down. That is happening, and will continue to happen. The thing you can control is your response to it. If you do control and shift your reaction, chances are you will get the outcome that is best for you. It would be beneficial when an event happens to put into practice a pause during which you take a moment to switch off the triggered response and say, "Okay, I am here now. This is happening. What's the message?" Anxiety tells you that you are experiencing things on a deep level, and that you are sensitive to life's trials and tribulations. The key is bringing about an awareness that clarifies what the anxiety is pointing to, and how you can change your attitude and response to whatever it is.

Those people, places and things that seem to create the anxiety are actually not manifesting it. You are. Your thoughts and responses spring from you, not whatever or whomever you are blaming. No one can "make" you feel hurt, angry or anxious. You are giving your mind permission to go into that emotion. You give the feeling your attention. We need to not only look at what we choose to give attention to as individuals, but also as a society. Fear and anxiety feeds on itself, and our planet becomes anxious. There's a choice, on a global scale, to either give attention to positivity or negativity. When we give energy to a collective positivity, we can change the world. We have to be open to the idea that challenges come to us not to hurt us, but to enlighten us. If we grasp at only what we think makes us happy, or have aversion and denial to our struggles, we end up in a state of anxiety or even physical illness.

The antidote to anxiety is the ability to neutralize it and focus the inner and outer essences of the mind. When you make a determined pledge to this Universe that you are ready to walk this path with full devotion, THEN your mind will begin to settle into the clear light of being. As long as you're scattered and unfocused, you're going to waiver. All the people around you and the events of your life are here for your enlightenment. If you see everything as having a higher order, you become more loving to yourself and others. Shooting the messenger of anxiety is not a way to stop the negative feelings. When you shoot that messenger, a whole new set of circumstances comes together once again, challenging you but offering another chance for enlightenment. Life causes anxiety and stress. Without it there would not be growth and learning. If you lean into it, you will understand that the struggle is your chance to evolve and to gain insight.

YOUR PAST – THE ROOTS OF ANXIETY

Your life from the start, along with the beginning of time for the Universe, is like a potter's wheel. It began to spin a very long time ago, and it is still in motion and will never stop. All that has happened in the past is applying itself and bearing down on you right now. How you react to it will create your future. You're not only dealing with what you did in your life, but also in past lives. When you know what the underlying cause or issue is of anxiety, you begin to learn to let it go.

There can be many levels of cause and effect in your life that have brought you to this point. When you take a deep look into your history, the journey is very much like an onion. You peel away a layer, then find another layer, and so on. There is energy still attached within these layers that needs to be recognized and processed. That is how peeling away at the past can result in enlightenment. The great thing about Spirit, the Universe, or whatever you want to call it, is that it never has, and never will, give you anything that you can't handle. It is within your power to determine what you will do with everything that happens to you. If you choose to see this truth, you'll find the gift of healing.

Anxiety can start when you are very young, even as an infant. Our connection and sensitivity to the world we come into and its circumstances can teach us anxiety, almost as a coping mechanism. If we don't feel secure, or nurtured, or loved, or understood, anxiety takes hold. In nature and human development, fear exists on a certain level to protect us from harmful things, but fear also exists in a larger harmful realm, where too many of us have been conditioned from a young age to feel fearful. Low-grade, constant anxiety can give us a false sense of security, as if worrying about it will control it somehow, but it actually has us acting and responding from a place of fear rather than love.

Do you have memories of one or both of your parents being anxious when you were young? Did they tell you about their problems in ways that may have made you feel burdened, unsafe, or guilty? Did they try to protect you from life's struggles, never giving you an opportunity to understand on an emotional level that there will always be positive and negative in life? Perhaps your parents put you in extremely competitive situations within the family dynamic or in school or sports. If you didn't "win" or achieve, you couldn't feel at peace. Did your parents have strong expectations of you that might not have lined up with who you really were/are? Anxiety can often trace its route back to different versions of these histories. Trauma is also how long-term anxiety breeds. If traumatic events in your past are not dealt with and are repressed, they are going to come out in any number of ways, with anxiety being a very common result.

Anxiety often feels like powerlessness. Think about your past, and who or what you felt was more powerful than you. What was the power dynamic in your family? Did you see power as something to be shared or as something to control other people with? Take a moment and form a picture of what power means to you. What does it look like? What does it feel like? When you recall these pictures are they positive pictures or are they negative pictures? Did power ever sound abusive to you? Or did it sound loving and supportive? What time in your life do you remember starting to feel anxiety? What happened then? How did the people around you behave? How were difficult or extreme events and situations handled? Did you learn that life would be a series of ups and downs, or was high drama and emotion an ever-present factor in your home?

We cannot undo the past, and in fact we need to accept the circumstances and in doing so understand what we were meant to learn in the process, and look further into what we gained from the experience. Looking at anxiety in your present life is a useful road map back to your past and the subconscious belief systems you adopted as a result of past experiences. How you cope with life's stresses and detours will determine how much, or how little, anxiety you feel. Peace is inside you, not in your external circumstances. Managing anxiety is impossible without self-reflection and eventual knowledge. And that is an ever-evolving process. Do you give and give and give of yourself, but neglect your own self-care? Do you avoid conflict? Are you fearful of the idea of your life taking a very different path than what you had planned? Have you not told those closest to you who you really are and what brings you joy? These are all different stories, yet they all share a high probability of pointing to something in your past. Reflecting and deconstructing the past can bring about anxiety for many, but the relief it provides once you have done it helps tremendously to lessen worry, angst and fear.

ANXIETY AND THE FEAR OF LACK

It is all too common for people to fear that they are going to lose what they have, or that they will never have what they need, and this can be the source of constant anxiety. The reality is that we need much less than we are led to believe. We will never be satisfied when we live in a state of anxiety over lack. Whether it is a big house, an expensive school for your kids, or a perfect mate, there's no true joy if you are scared that your joy is based on those external things. The cycle of grasping and chasing leaves no room for perspective, gratitude, and inner peace. If anxiety is the theme music playing in the background of your life, you won't be able to hear your own mind asking you to reflect and find answers from within. The anticipation of what is going to happen, or not happen, is one of the core elements of anxiety. As much as we know that worry and fear are not going to change anything, and in fact will probably make coping more difficult, we go down that road. Our culture, with its messaging, ever-present social media and societal pressure, feeds the idea that your life is not as exciting, abundant or important as it should be.

Anxiety keeps you from claiming what life has to offer for you. When you can't accept all the potential the Universe has for you, you worry about losing what you have now. Once you realize you have anxiety over food, money, love, or anything else, what are the steps you can take to overcome it and trust that the Universe/God/Source will replenish itself? There are unlimited possibilities for you in the world, especially when you are facing huge challenges. The same is true when small things are bringing about your anxiety. Things change and shift across the spectrum. Jobs and careers change, relationships change, and where you live can change. On a smaller scale, the traffic jam that's making you anxious will change, and the test or public speaking obligation that you're having anxiety over will be done at some point. Anxiety rarely sees the flow of change that we all live with. It forgets that life is a continuum, not a stagnant situation. Keeping perspective is a state of mindfulness that anxiety stands in the way of.

The kind of anxiety that hums along in the background of your life is the most difficult to call out and address. An anxiety attack that is obvious in its severity is hard to ignore and can force us to take action for self-care and outside help. But quiet, low-grade anxiety can be harming you without your awareness. Some people may not even know they are anxious. Understanding how fear of loss, or of not receiving something we think is vital to happiness, can shape our reactions and responses to life is vital to unveiling anxiety. Feeling anxious mutes your inherent power and makes you vulnerable. You are more likely to experience self-doubt, hurt and victimhood, among other negative emotions when you are anxious. Your actions and decisions might be heavily influenced by anxiety. Stop the next time before you respond to something that happens during your day. Are you reacting from a space of anxiety and the fear that surrounds it, or from a space of empowerment?

We inadvertently become the emotions we are feeling, even though they are not our truth. You are not your anxiety. Anxiety is a feeling that flows through you once you understand and know how to process it. Letting go of negative feelings can be so difficult for the very reason that we often have come to identify ourselves as that feeling. Because anxiety can be long-term and pervasive it's common to hear, "I'm an anxious person." You may very well be a sensitive person and/or someone who thinks very deeply, and anxiety is not part of your essential spirit. It does not have to define you. You need faith – in whatever form that it manifests for you – to tackle anxious feelings. You need faith that things will change, to accept that challenging situations arise at times, that loss and gain are inevitable and outside of your control, and that worry and fear never stop what is going to happen, or not happen. That's how the universe works.

ANXIETY IN A CHAOTIC WORLD – ACCEPTANCE, HEALING AND HOPE

There's a lot of anxiety in the world right now. Worry about the future, violence, uncertainty, hardship, and justice occupy our minds. Though it makes perfect sense that we would have worry and fear, how can you learn to keep it in check, find a place of peace, and transform anxiety into positive energy and action? The weight of the world is not yours to bear. Nothing can change within yourself, nor can you impact the world around you if you are locked in your own prison of anxiety. Caring about the state of the world is not the same as having anxiety about it. Care and empathy will propel you into a mindset that can be a positive force. Anxiety just paralyzes you and creates inaction and inward thinking that feeds on itself.

You cannot be of service to others by feeling anxious about their circumstances, or your own. Acceptance doesn't mean complacency, yet you cannot fight the good fight until you see the positive and negative elements in the world as part of a natural order. There will be light and there will be dark. All the anxiety in the universe won't change anyone's situation, or an issue, or unfair policy, or wrongdoing at any level. When we work on our own consciousness, we can then connect with a collective consciousness that can transform people, countries and the entire world. Healing begins with self-reflection and discovery.

Mindfulness is the counterbalance to anxiety in both our individual lives and our connection to our world. We can use the past as a guide by gaining wisdom from what has happened to us – and to us as a society/

world. We can also hold a vision of a future to use as a road map that we put our full intention into following. Yet, being present and living in the moment is where we must come back to and ground ourselves. You cannot change the past or have set expectations of the future. Mindfulness allows you to recognize the anxiety you are feeling – and the anxiety that others are feeling also – with acceptance and focus that ultimately makes it much easier to turn into empowerment. We cannot take up residence in the past or the future. If there is something you want to change, you start by changing your thinking. When you live with mindfulness you see anxiety as just a feeling, not something that you should grasp onto. When you live in the present, you see the bigger picture and the hope that exists even in the darkest hour.

Quieting anxiety is a quieting of the mind. All of us need to begin to take responsibility for who we are, what we are, and what it is that we want to change. To get there you have to come from a space of silence. At some stage, we must make a conscious decision to say, "Okay, here I am, I am sitting here. I'm going to be quiet for a moment and I'm going to see what is going on in my life right now that could be changed for the better." You are inherently empowered to understand that no matter what emotion you are feeling, it's all energy at the end of the day. How much energy you put into feeling anxious about the world, or your individual life, will determine whether it lives or whether it dies. If you plant a vegetable in the garden and you don't water it and give it nourishment, it will die, simple as that. You have to cut off the life force of anything you don't want in your life anymore, or it's going to continue to grow. The first step is to acknowledge that anxiety is keeping you from experiencing all the potential that is available to you. Once you recognize that anxiety has become an issue, you can begin to take away its life force.

Extreme anxiety, whether about external factors or from the circumstances of your life, can cause panic attacks. Some are small and pass quickly; others are full-blown and manifest dramatic physical symptoms like heart palpitations, headaches, stomach problems, muddled or disoriented thinking, and uncontrollable fear. A panic attack can grip you before you are about to do something you dread, or in advance of seeing a person you'd rather avoid. Some people seem more predisposed to panic attacks, but everyone can benefit from starting a spiritual or mindfulness practice that grounds you in your own consciousness – not in the external factors of life, no matter how dark – and shows you that there is a choice as to how you focus your thoughts and feelings. Peace of mind is about taking things as they come.

In order to shape your future, you have to be able to let go and experience everything without judgment. Anxiety manifests when we are stuck in thinking there's a way that things should be and how events should happen. There's no controlling anything that is outside of your own mind and behavior. The burden of expectations quietly chips away at your potential. Living in a world filled with anxiety can be overwhelming. Social media and the pressures of our society have only made things more difficult to navigate. We are comparing ourselves to others, grasping at fleeting things, and in denial over challenging, yet regularly occurring circumstances and situations. The natural order is disorder, except when it comes to our training, our mindset, and opening our heart to compassion.

PRACTICAL TIPS TO COMBAT ANXIETY

Here are some of the things you can put into practice to reduce anxiety in your life, gain self-awareness, and realize your potential.

- Be present and live in the moment. Treat the past and the future as part of the continuum of the present. The past informs us and the future inspires us, but the "now" is all that truly matters. When feeling anxiety over the past or the future, bring yourself back to this moment and clear your mind.

- Observe your habits and patterns. What can you do to redirect them? It starts with small steps. It is too overwhelming to expect radical change immediately. Be aware of your triggers and how you react.

- Are you anxious because you are suppressing your true nature? Are you hiding things about yourself because you are afraid of rejection or judgment? Have you let go of what you are passionate about? Be true to yourself. Get back to who you want to be.

- Tap into your spirituality, higher power, teachings, nature or mindfulness practice – whatever connects you to the Universe.

- Stop complaining about your situation – change what you can but most importantly, change your attitude.

- Don't act just to act. Sometimes doing nothing is the right thing.

- Stop comparing yourself to others and work on reversing feeling "less than."

- Remember that everything is impermanent and always changing.

- Do you have anxiety about what you regret having done or not done in your life? Or about things you feel you could have done differently? Let go of the idea that you have fallen short or will fail in the future. Your legacy is how you live your life, how you love, how you help rather than hurt. Not external achievements, fame or wealth.

- Keep perspective – are the things you think to be important really important? Do you overreact, or do you act proportionally to the situation? The gift of having struggled in life is that it informs you and gives you the knowledge that the natural order is that there will be dark and light, positive and negative.

- Stop looking outside of yourself – you are not defined by your work, relationships, or public image. If you are constantly chasing the external, nothing will ever be satisfying.

- Stop thinking you need to "fix" everything.

- Don't have expectations. Allow space for a different path to reveal itself.

- Look at the role of anger in your life. Is your anxiety actually anger that you have turned back in on itself?

- Work on self-awareness. Ground your consciousness in reality, not a skewed vision of yourself and the world.

- Resist the feeling that you are missing something all the time. You are where you are meant to be in this moment.

- Stop blaming – when we experience anxiety, we struggle to find someone or something to blame. We assume that there must be some external reason we are feeling this bad, and that if we just remove that situation, we will be okay. Sometimes there is an external cause, but there are many situations we may not be able to do much about, no matter how stressful they may be.

- Are you stretched too thin in your responsibilities for parenting and/or work? Accept that there may not be enough time in the day for all you need to do, but find the best possible solutions to not feeling burned out. Share childcare with a friend so you can have a break. Talk to your boss about your job duties and see if there can be adjustments.

- Avoid over-scheduling – this is a major source of anxiety in our society. Children in particular are growing up with anxiety caused by too many activities with high parental expectations and pressures at school to do well. Enjoy downtime and teach your children to do the same.

- Look into time management help/skills. Money and organizational management programs or classes can give you tools to make you feel less anxious. Declutter your home.

- Learn to relax, even if you can only fit in short spurts during the day. Carve out a block of time.

- Stop saying, "I have to" ("I have to do that extra work") and "but" ("I'd take a walk, but…."). Say, "I will" and "I want to."

- Look at what role guilt plays in your life. Try to see how it could be connected to anxiety.

- Pay attention to your dreams – dreams can release anxiety about waking life and work out things on a subconscious level. Make a suggestion to yourself before you go to sleep, "I will remember my dreams." Keep a journal or notepad near your bed and write down your dreams right away for analysis later.

- Watch your diet, eat healthy, exercise, practice stress relievers such as yoga, meditation, and mindfulness. Get enough sleep.

- As much as you can, keep away from people and situations that make you anxious.

- Slow down!

- Don't go into dread and anxiety over holidays, family stress, events, tests, or job reviews. Deal with what you must but don't decide beforehand what something or someone is going to be like or do. Realize that anxious feelings will do nothing to help you get through in the most positive light.

- Practice gratitude. Be mindful of what you have to be grateful for. Keep a gratitude list.

- Break away from materialism as much as you can. A simpler life can be a fuller life that results in less anxiety.

- Turn off the media, including social

media. Unplug! You don't need to know everything, all the time. Especially if it ends up making you feel anxious.

- Tap into books or quotes that inspire you. Keep the ones that most resonate on a chalkboard, on your computer screen saver, posted on the refrigerator, or in your wallet.

- Draw, paint, create. Enjoy nature. Have fun with people.

- Seek professional help when you need it.

- Practice service to others, good deeds are an antidote to anxiety.

MEDITATION TO EASE ANXIETY

Meditation is a very effective tool for easing anxiety and anxious feelings. A regular practice that reinforces the peacefulness you achieve from meditation can teach you a new way of processing stress, worry, and trauma. Here is a great meditation that focuses on inner peace, reflection, and deep connection with a higher power:

Find a quiet spot where you won't be disturbed. Make yourself as comfortable as you can and take two or three slow, deep breaths. As you exhale on the third breath, close your eyes, relax, and let go. Let the events of the day float away, along with obligations that are on your mind. For the next 15-20 minutes (or more) nobody wants or expects anything from you. There's nothing whatsoever for you to do except to just relax. Allow your mind to settle into that space of peace. This is the time for you to just switch off from the world.

Now, imagine that there's a gold orb of bright light right over your head. It looks like the sun when it's rising in the morning – or setting in the evening. I want you to feel the warmth of that sun and imagine now that this gold orb is resting gently on the top of your head, drifting gently like warm honey-colored grains growing in a field. Rest your mind on that orb and let it flow now down from your head, into your neck, into your throat, and feel it begin to spread across your shoulders. Its warmth is healing, eliminating anxiety, worry and stress.

Imagine the light rolling down your shoulders and into your arms, gently caressing, healing, soothing and relaxing your entire being. The warm gold light travels through your body, into your elbows, your forearms, wrists, hands and fingers. From your shoulders the light begins to seep into your chest, eliminating any source of stress that you may have picked up throughout the day or in the past week. The orb drifts down into your chest, into your abdomen, relaxing, caressing and caring for you. This gold light is like having an old friend return to you, filling the trunk of your body as it now reaches your hips. Again, feel the warmth of this healing gold light as it begins to flow from your hips into the top of your legs, from your legs down to your knees, taking all the time in the world. It cannot be rushed. It just gently flows at its own pace, a bit like watching honey drip off a spoon. Down your shins, your calves, into your ankles, into your feet and toes, and then going through your being into Mother Earth, carrying with it any fears or hurts that you may have experienced in your life. Mother Earth is receiving all your hurts and just transforming them back into love and light.

As you just sit quietly now, completely calm and relaxed, I'd like you to imagine that two guardian angels have come and are standing behind you. If there are issues in your life that you feel you might need help with, now is the time to ask these two guardian angels to guide you. Knowing that when you request it, it will be done, trusting that these angels are now and always will be around you, showing up from time to time in your life as other beings. Imagine that these angels now are making representations on your behalf to the universe, to the world, and to everybody in it, to leave you in peace. To let you have peace, feel peace, and be peace. See these angels send gold light from their heart to your heart, taking away any sadness, any fears, any resentments, disappointments or grudges that you may have experienced in the last while. Feel these emotions lift off of your being.

And now, as you're in this wise space of your own being, apply the teaching that says the best way to end trouble is to send love. Imagine a gold light coming from your heart to people, situations and experiences that you need to change in your life. Let the gold light go from you to them. If you find it difficult to send this loving gold light at this time, imagine the two angels are sending it for you on your behalf. Sending it to people who might have hurt you in the past – people who don't understand you. Then bringing it back to yourself, to be enveloped with self-acceptance and love.

They say that that which you want the most you must give away. If you are looking for love, you must give love away. If you are looking for wealth, you must give wealth away. By giving it away, you energize the circle of light, and that circle of light will always return to its source. What you give out is what you receive. Always remember, when you sit in the quiet space of your mind, you will always be safe and secure. You will always be improving your health and wellbeing. Send this peace and quiet to all beings in this world so they experience the happiness of oneness, the happiness that brings us together to learn from each other. When we come together, we learn much more deeply than when we're alone.

Try to take some time out every day. If you find it difficult to meditate, you can just light a candle and sit and watch it for five minutes. You will find this easy practice to be very beneficial. Your anxiety will disappear and abundance of all kinds will begin to flow into your life. Bliss can become a natural part of your life.

Now, at the count of five, open your eyes, stay relaxed and at peace, and notice how aware you feel of the world and everything in it.

ABOUT THE AUTHOR

Fondly referred to as the Celtic Sage, Irish-born spiritual teacher Derek O'Neill inspires and uplifts people from all walks of life, offering guidance to influential world leaders, businesses, celebrities, athletes and everyday people alike. Distilled from his life work in psychotherapy, a martial arts career and study with wise yogis and Indian and Tibetan masters, Derek translates ancient wisdom into modern day teachings to address the biggest challenges facing humanity today.

For more than 30 years, Derek O'Neill has been transforming the lives of thousands of people around the world through workshops, consultations, speaking engagements, media, and tireless humanitarian work.

Drawing on years of training in martial arts, which earned him the level of Master

Black Belt, coupled with his extraordinary intuitive abilities and expertise as a psychotherapist, Derek has pioneered a new psychology, transformational therapy. His signature process, aptly named "The Sword and the Brush," helps clients to seamlessly transmute their struggles into positive outcomes, using the sword to cut away old patterns and the brush to help paint the picture of the new life that they require.

Inspired by his worldly travels, Derek and his late wife Linda formed SQ Foundation, a not-for-profit organization focused on helping to solve global issues facing humanity today. In recognition of his service, Derek was honored with the highly prestigious Variety International Humanitarian Award, Arts for India Dayawati Modi Global Award, Irish Autism Action Man of the Year, and Hearts and Minds Pride of Eireann. Derek currently serves on the Board of Directors at Variety International.

Author of More Truth Will Set You Free, the Get a Grip series of pocket books, a cutting edge book on parenting titled Calm Mama, Happy Baby, and several children's books, Derek also hosted his own radio show, "The Way With Derek O'Neill," which enjoyed the most successful launch in VoiceAmerica's history, quickly garnering 100,000 listeners.

To learn more about Derek O'Neill, to attend his next workshops, to order books, download teachings, or to contact him, please visit his website: **derekoneill.com**

To learn more about SQ Foundation, the global charity that is changing the lives of hundreds of thousands of people around the world, go to: **sq-foundation.org**

RESOURCES

'Get a Grip' Book Series

Abundance: Starts Right Now

Addiction: What a Cover-Up!

Anger: Who Gives a Shite?

Anxiety: To Peace

Bullying: You Won't Beat Me

Confidence: Easy For You to Say

Consciousness: It's All Over You

Depression: What's that?

Desire: Never Fulfilled but Grows

Dreams: The Best Messengers

Excellence: You Never Lost It, You Forgot It

Fear: A Powerful Illusion

Forgiveness: So I Can Move On

Gratitude: Yes Please

Grief: Mind Boggling But Natural

Happiness: You Must Be Effin' Joking!

Love/Divorce: Soulmate or Cellmate?

Mindfulness: Out Of Or In Your Mind?

Relationships: Would You Want to Date You?

Stress: Is Stress Stressing You Out?

Suicide: Fast or Slow

Weight: What's Eating You?

Other Books
More Truth Will Set You Free
Calm Mama, Happy Baby

Children's Books
Water Drop Coloring Book
The Adventures of Lucinda in Love-Filled Fairyland

www.ingramcontent.com/pod-product-compliance
Lightning Source LLC
Chambersburg PA
CBHW071541080526
44588CB00011B/1739